Other books in this series:
Thank Heavens for Friends
To my Grandmother with Love
For Mother a Gift of Love
To my Daughter with Love

For My Father
Marriage a Keepsake
Words of Comfort

EDITED BY HELEN EXLEY
BORDERS BY SHARON BASSIN

Published simultaneously in 1993 by Exley Publications in
Great Britain, and Exley Giftbooks in the USA.

12   11   10   9   8   7

Picture and text selection by © Helen Exley 1993.
Border Illustrations © Sharon Bassin 1993.
The moral right of the author has been asserted.

ISBN 1-85015-453-8

Picture research by Image Select International.
Typeset by Brush Off, St. Albans.
Printed in China.

Exley Publications Ltd, 16 Chalk Hill, Watford,
Herts WD1 4BN, United Kingdom.

Exley Giftbooks, 232 Madison Avenue, Suite 1206,
NY 10016, USA.

ℒOVE

A CELEBRATION

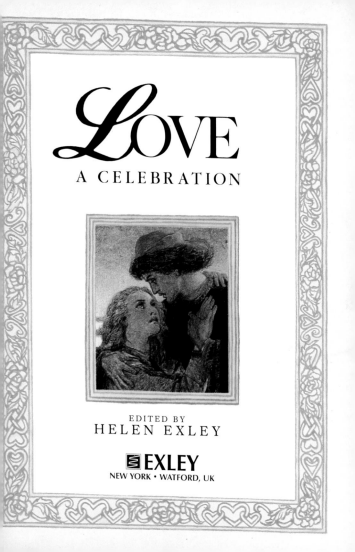

EDITED BY
HELEN EXLEY

≣ **EXLEY**
NEW YORK • WATFORD, UK

. . . and then I asked him with my eyes
and then he asked me would I yes . . .
and first I put my arms around him yes
and drew him down to me
to ask again yes
so he could feel my breasts all perfume yes
and his heart was going like mad
and yes I said yes I will Yes.

JAMES JOYCE
FROM ULYSSES

ALWAYS MARRY AN APRIL GIRL

Praise the spells and bless the charms,
I found April in my arms.
April golden, April cloudy.
Gracious, cruel, tender, rowdy;
April soft in flowered langor
April cold with sudden anger,
Ever changing, ever true –
I love April. I love you.

OGDEN NASH

(i do not know what it is about you that closes
and opens;only something in me understands
the voice of your eyes is deeper than all roses)

E.E. CUMMINGS

THE POWER OF LOVE

Across the gateway of my heart
  I wrote "No thoroughfare,"
But love came laughing by, and cried
  "I enter everywhere".

HERBERT SHIPMAN

There is no greater wonder than the way the
face of a young woman fits in a man's mind, and
stays there, and he could never tell you why; it
just seems it was the thing he wanted.

ROBERT LOUIS STEVENSON, CATRIONA

ALL I ASK –

All I ask of a woman is that she shall feel gently
    towards me
when my heart feels kindly towards her,
and there shall be the soft, soft tremor as of unheard
    bells between us.
It is all I ask.
I am so tired of violent women lashing out
    and insisting on being loved, when there is
    no love in them.

D.H. Lawrence

DAYBREAK

At dawn she lay with her profile at that angle
Which, when she sleeps, seems the carved face
    of an angel.
Her hair a harp, the hand of a breeze follows
And plays, against the white cloud of the pillows.
Then, in a flush of rose, she woke, and her eyes
    that opened
Swam in blue through her rose flesh that dawned.
"My dream becomes my dream," she said, "come true.
I waken from you to my dream of you."
Oh, my own wakened dream then dared assume
The audacity of her sleep. Our dreams
Poured into each other's arms, like streams.

STEPHEN SPENDER

Drink to me only with thine eyes,
    And I will pledge with mine;
Or leave a kiss but in the cup
    And I'll not look for wine.
The thirst that from the soul doth rise
    Doth ask a drink divine;
But might I of Jove's nectar sup,
    I would not change for thine.

I sent thee late a rosy wreath,
    Not so much honouring thee
As giving it a hope that there
    It could not withered be;
But thou thereon didst only breathe
    And sent'st it back to me;
Since when it grows, and smells, I swear,
    Not of itself but thee!

BEN JONSON

SHE WALKS IN BEAUTY

She walks in Beauty, like the night
    Of cloudless climes and starry skies;
And all that's best of dark and bright
    Meet in her aspect and her eyes:
Thus mellowed to that tender light
    Which Heaven to gaudy day denies.

One shade the more, one ray the less,
    Had half impaired the nameless grace
Which waves in every raven tress,
    Or softly lightens o'er her face;
Where thoughts serenely sweet express
    How pure, how dear their dwelling-place.

And on that cheek, and o'er that brow,
    So soft, so calm, yet eloquent,
The smiles that win, the tints that glow,
    But tell of days in goodness spent,
A mind at peace with all below
    A heart whose love is innocent!

LORD BYRON

"May I print a kiss on your lips?" I said,
  And she nodded her full permission;
So we went to press and I rather guess
  We printed a full edition.

JOSEPH LILIENTHAL

I gently touched her hand: she gave
A look that did my soul enslave;
I pressed her rebel lips in vain;
They rose up to be pressed again.
    Thus happy, I no farther meant,
    Than to be pleased and innocent.

On her soft breasts my hand I laid,
And a quick, light impression made;
They with a kindly warmth did glow,
And swelled, and seemed to overflow.
    Yet, trust me, I no farther meant,
    Than to be pleased and innocent.

On her eyes my eyes did stay:
O'er her smooth limbs my hands did stray;
Each sense was ravished with delight,
And my soul stood prepared for flight.
    Blame me not if at last I meant
    More to be pleased than innocent.

ANON

TO MY VALENTINE

More than a catbird hates a cat,
Or a criminal hates a clue,
Or the Axis hates the United States,
That's how much I love you.

I love you more than a duck can swim,
And more than a grapefruit squirts,
I love you more than gin rummy is a bore,
And more than a toothache hurts.

As a shipwrecked sailor hates the sea,
Or a juggler hates a shove,
As a hostess detests unexpected guests,
That's how much you I love.

I love you more than a wasp can sting,
And more than the subway jerks,
I love you as much as a beggar needs a crutch,
And more than a hangnail irks.

I swear to you by the stars above,
And below, if such there be,
As the High Court loathes perjurious oaths,
That's how you're loved by me.

Ogden Nash

mr youse needn't be so spry
concernin questions arty

each has his tastes but as for i
i likes a certain party

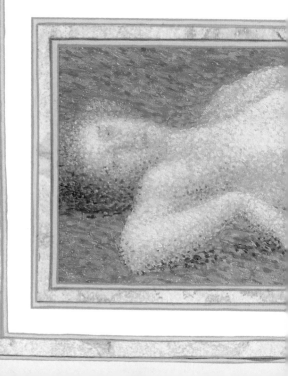

gimme the he-man's solid bliss
for youse ideas i'll match youse

a pretty girl who naked is
is worth a million statues

E.E. CUMMINGS

How fair and how pleasant art thou, O love,
For delights!
This thy stature is like to a palm tree,
And thy breasts to clusters of grapes.
I said, I will go up to the palm tree,
I will take hold of the boughs thereof:
Now also thy breasts shall be
As clusters of the vine,
And the smell of thy nose like apples;
And the roof of thy mouth
Like the best wine for my beloved,
That goeth down sweetly,
Causing the lips of those that are asleep
To speak.
I am my beloved's,
And his desire is toward me . . .

THE SONG OF SONGS

ALTHOUGH I CONQUER ...

Although I conquer all the earth,
yet for me there is only one city.
In that city there is for me only one house;
And in that house, one room only;
And in that room, a bed.
And one woman sleeps there,
The shining joy and jewel of all my kingdom.

FROM THE SANSKRIT

may my heart always be open to little
birds who are the secrets of living
whatever they sing is better than to know
and if men should not hear them men are old

may my mind stroll about hungry
and fearless and thirsty and supple
and even if it's sunday may i be wrong
for whenever men are right they are not young

and may myself do nothing usefully
and love yourself so more than truly
there's never been quite such a fool who could fail
pulling all the sky over him with one smile

E.E. CUMMINGS

THE LOOK

Strephon kissed me in the Spring,
   Robin in the fall,
But Colin only looked at me
   And never kissed at all.

Strephon's kiss was lost in jest,
   Robin's lost in play,
But the kiss in Colin's eyes
   Haunts me night and day.

SARA TEASDALE

BY CHANCE

I'd have been all right
If you hadn't smiled
Lighting your eyes on to mine

But since you did
And we spoke and touched
I've another dream
I've conflict
And loss

ELSPETH SANDYS

love is more thicker than forget
more thinner than recall
more seldom than a wave is wet
more frequent than to fail

it is most mad and moonly
and less it shall unbe
than all the sea which only
is deeper than the sea

love is less always than to win
less never than alive
less bigger than the least begin
less littler than forgive

it is most sane and sunly
and more it cannot die
than all the sky which only
is higher than the sky

E.E. CUMMINGS

DESTINY

Somewhere there waiteth in this
    world of ours
For one lone soul another lonely soul,
Each choosing each through all the
    weary hours
And meeting strangely at one sudden
    goal.
Then blend they, like green leaves
    with golden flowers,
Into one beautiful and perfect whole;
And life's long night is ended, and the
    way
Lies open onward to eternal day.

EDWIN ARNOLD

Only of thee and me the nightwind sings:
    Only of us the lovers speak at sea;
The earth is full of breathless whisperings
    Only of thee and me.

Only of thee and me the forests chant;
    Only of us the stir in bush and tree;
The rain and sun inform the blossoming plant
    Only of thee and me.

Only of thee and me till all shall fade;
    Only of us the world's first thought can be;
For we are love, and heaven itself is made
    Only of thee and me.

LOUIS UNTERMEYER

BARGAIN

I'd gladly lose me to find you,
I'd gladly give up all I had,
To find you I'd suffer anything
And be glad.

I'd pay any price just to get you,
I'd work all my life, and I will.
To win you I'd stand naked,
Stoned and stabbed,
I'd call that a bargain,
The best I ever had,
The best I ever had.

I'd gladly lose me to find you,
I'd gladly give up all I got,
To catch you I'm gonna run
And never stop.

I'd pay any price just to win you,
Surrender my good life for bad.
To find you I'm gonna drown
An unsung man,
I'd call that a bargain,
The best I ever had,
The best I ever had.

I sit looking round,
I look at the face in the mirror.
I know I'm worth nothing
Without you,
And like one and one
Don't make two;
One and one make one,
And I'm looking for
That free ride to me,
I'm looking
For you.

PETE TOWNSHEND

The fountains mingle with the river
   And the rivers with the Ocean,
The Winds of Heaven mix for ever
   With a sweet emotion;
Nothing in the world is single;
   All things by a law divine
In one spirit meet and mingle.
   Why not I with thine?

See the mountains kiss high Heaven
    And the waves clasp one another;
No sister-flower would be forgiven
    If it disdained its brother;
And the sunlight clasps the earth
    And the moonbeams kiss the sea:
What is all this sweet work worth
    If thou kiss not me?

PERCY BYSSHE SHELLEY

CELIA CELIA

When I am sad and weary,
When I think all hope has gone,
When I walk along High Holborn
I think of you with nothing on.

ADRIAN MITCHELL

MY LOVE IS LIKE A RED RED ROSE

My love is like a red red rose
    That's newly sprung in June:
My love is like the melody
    That's sweetly play'd in tune.

As fair art thou, my bonnie lass,
    So deep in love am I;
And I will love thee still, my dear,
    Till a' the seas gang dry.

Till a' the seas gang dry, my dear,
    And the rocks melt wi' the sun:
And I will love thee still, my dear,
    While the sands o' life shall run.

And fare thee weel, my only love,
    And fare thee weel a while!
And I will come again, my love,
    Tho' it were ten thousand mile.

ROBERT BURNS

Good-night? ah! no; the hour is ill
    Which severs those it should unite;
Let us remain together still,
    Then it will be good night.

How can I call the lone night good,
    Though thy sweet wishes wing its flight?
Be it not said, thought, understood,
    Then it will be good night.

To hearts which near each other move
    From evening close to morning light,
The night is good; because, my love
    They never say good-night.

PERCY BYSSHE SHELLEY

BROWN PENNY

I whispered "I am too young,"
And then, "I am old enough";
Wherefore I threw a penny
To find out if I might love.
"Go and love, go and love, young man,
If the lady be young and fair."
Ah, penny, brown penny, brown penny,
I am looped in the loops of her hair.

O love is the crooked thing,
There is nobody wise enough.
To find out all that is in it,
For he would be thinking of love
Till the stars had run away
And the shadows eaten the moon.
Ah, penny, brown penny, brown penny,
One cannot begin it too soon.

W.B. Yeats

NIGHT

The night has a thousand eyes,
   And the day but one;
Yet the light of the bright world dies
   With the dying sun.

The mind has a thousand eyes,
   And the heart but one;
Yet the light of a whole life dies,
   When love is done.

FRANCIS WILLIAM BOURDILLON

WE'LL GO NO MORE A-ROVING

So, we'll go no more a-roving
   So late into the night,
Though the heart be still as loving,
   And the moon be still as bright.

For the sword outwears its sheath,
   And the soul wears out the breast,
And the heart must pause to breathe,
   And love itself have rest.

Though the night was made for loving,
   And the day returns too soon,
Yet we'll go no more a-roving
   By the light of the moon.

LORD BYRON

JENNY KISSED ME

Jenny kissed me when we met,
    Jumping from the chair she sat in;
Time, you thief ! who love to get
    Sweets into your list, put that in:
Say I'm weary, say I'm sad,
    Say that health and wealth have missed me,
Say I'm growing old, but add, –
    Jenny kissed me.

LEIGH HUNT

O WESTERN WIND

O western wind, when wilt thou blow
    That the small rain down can rain?
Christ, if my love were in my arms,
    And I in my bed again.

ANON

Acknowledgements: The publishers gratefully acknowledge permission to reproduce copyright material, and would be interested to hear from any copyright holders not here acknowledged.
E.E. CUMMINGS: "(i do not know what ...", from 'somewhere i have never travelled gladly beyond' is reprinted from *Viva*, poems by E . E . Cummings, by permission of Liveright Publishing Corporation. © 1931, 1959 by E.E. Cummings. © 1979, 1973 by Nancy T. Andrews. © 1979, 1973 by George James Firmage; © 1979 by the Trustees for the E. E. Cummings trust, reproduced with the permission of W.W. Norton & Co; "mr youse needn' t be so spry" is reprinted from *IS 5*, poems by E. E. Cummings, by permission of Liveright Publishing Corporation. © 1926 by Horace Liveright. Copyright renewed 1953 by E.E. Cummings; © 1967 by Marion Morehouse Cummings and "may my heart always be open to little", © 1938 by e.e. cummings; © 1966 by Marion Morehouse Cummings by permission of Liveright Publishing Corporation and W.W. Norton & Co; JAMES JOYCE: extract from *Ulysses*, published by The Bodley Head and Random House, Inc. D.H. LAWRENCE: "All I Ask" from *The Complete Poems of D.H. Lawrence*, edited by Vivian de Sola Pinto and F. Warren Roberts. Copyright © 1964, 1971 by Angelo Ravagli and C.M. Weekley, Executors of the Estate of Frieda Lawrence Ravagli. Used by permission of Laurence Pollinger Ltd and Viking Penguin, a division of Penguin Books USA Inc; ADRIAN MITCHELL: "Celia, Celia", from *Out Loud*, reprinted with permission of the author; OGDEN NASH: "Always Marry An April Girl" and "To My Valentine" from *I Wouldn' t Have Missed It* by Ogden Nash. Copyright 1942, 1943 by Ogden Nash. Reprinted by permission of Little, Brown and Company and Curtis Brown Ltd. ELSPETH SANDYS: "By Chance", reprinted by permission of the author; STEPHEN SPENDER: "Daybreak" from *Collected Poems 1928-1953* and Ruins and Visions, © 1942 and 1970 by Stephen Spender, reprinted by permission of the publishers, Faber and Faber Ltd and Random House, Inc ; SARA TEASDALE: "The Look" from *Collected Poems 1928-1953*, © 1915 by Macmillan Publishing Co. Inc, renewed 1943 by Mamie T. Wheless. Reprinted with permission of Macmillan Publishing Co. Inc; PETE TOWNSHEND: "Bargain", reprinted with permission of the author and Fabulous Music Ltd; W.B. YEATS: "Brown Penny", from *Collected Poems* © 1912 Macmillan Publishing Co. Inc, renewed 1940 by Bertha Georgie Yeats, reprinted by permission of Macmillan Publishing Co. Inc.
Picture Credits: Bridgeman Art Library: title page and pages 6, 19 © Emile J.J. Simon, "An Odalisque" - John Noot Galeries, 25 © Dora Holzhandler, "Lovers in Holland Park", 26, 30, 33, 35, 37, 39, 41, 47 © Lucien Levy-Dhurmer (1865 - 1943), 49 by courtesy of the Board of Trustees of The Victoria & Albert Museum, London 53 © Nikolai Novikov (b.1922) "The Poet, Sergei Esenin" 1975, 56, 59 Giraudon © Andre Collin (b.1862), "Poor People"; Hessisches Landesmuseum Darmstadt: page 6; Fine Art Photographic Library Ltd: pages 8/9, 12, 54; AKG: cover and pages 10, 15, 16, 20, 22, 28, 43 © Willi Balendat (1901-1969) "Die Nachigall, Forster-Dulles-Weg Berlin" 1963, 50/51 © DACS 1993, Edvard Munch "The Kiss" 1892, National Gallery, Oslo, 60/61; The Israel Museum, Jerusalem: page 10; Whitford & Hughes, London: page 26, 35, 47; Osterreichisches Gallerie, Vienna: pages 28, 37; Birmingham City Museum & Art Gallery: page 30; City of Bristol Museum & Art Gallery: page 41; Scala: page 44/45; Galleria d'Arte Moderna, Roma: page 44/45; Musee Des Beaux-Arts, Tournai: page 59.